scrapbooking

BEST OF FRIENDS

Ashton got the movie 101 Dalmations off the Easter bunny ever since then he's been Dalmation crazy, so when he got 'Brodie' he was one happy little boy, he just loves to play 'catch with him'

scrapbooking

Jayne
Bentley

Published by SILVERDALE BOOKS
An imprint of Bookmart Ltd
Registered number 2372865
Trading as Bookmart Ltd
Blaby Road
Wigston
Leicester LE18 4SE

2006 D&S Books Ltd

©D&S Books Ltd
Kerswell,
Parkham Ash, Bideford
Devon, England
EX39 5PR

e-mail us at:- enquiries@d-sbooks.co.uk

This edition printed 2006

ISBN 1-84509-296-1

DS0110. Scrapbooking

Creative Director: Sarah King
Editor: Debbie Key
Project editor: Judith Millidge
Designer: 2H Design

Typeset in Helvetica and Goudy
Printed in Thailand

1 3 5 7 9 10 8 6 4 2

Contents

An introduction to scrapbooking

What is it about a photograph that draws you in and keeps you wanting to share it with friends and family?

To me it's all about the memory. I take photos of all the important events such as births, weddings, first day of school, but it's often the images of every day life that are my favourite. The look of pure enjoyment on my daughter's face as she sits on a swing. The tender embrace of my father-in-law holding my son, or both children jumping up and down on the trampoline with their dog. All of these memories tell the stories of our lives. Some make us smile, some make us misty-eyed and some just make us laugh out loud.

So why is it, that more often than not, these memories just get placed in a draw, a container or even a shoe box?

Many people, though, do have good intentions and create wedding albums, or fill in a baby's first year book. When these are completed, they are far more enjoyable to look through than just flicking through a pile of random photos.

One of my favourite pastimes as a child, was to sit with my mum on a Sunday afternoon and pour over the albums that she had created, affectionately called *Books of Remembrance*. They fascinated me.

I loved looking at photos of people I had never met, especially my great-granddad. I always wanted to know what he was like as I had heard such wonderful stories about him from my grandmother. She always put on a Cockney accent when she told those stories as he was from London. I remember looking at my hospital ID tag wondering if my wrists could ever have been that tiny – Mum would always assure me I was. The thing I liked best was to read the precious pages Mum had typed about my life. All the funny sayings I had, my first word and my imaginary friend who happened to be a witch that lived in a water tower!

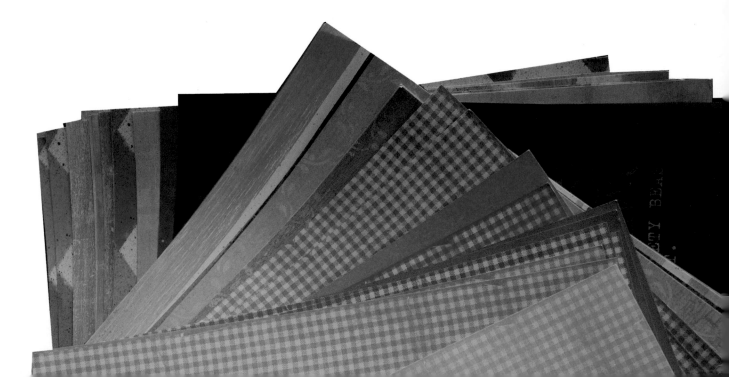

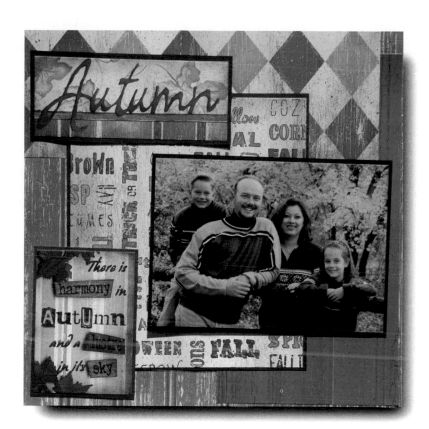

When I discovered scrapbooking I thought I'd gone to heaven, having found a new creative outlet to incorporate the photographs and record the stories of my life. It also makes me happy and reminds me just how blessed I really am.

The books my mum created are now starting to show their age. The glues which were used no longer hold the photos. The tape that was used to hold some items down has now turned yellow and become brittle, as have the newspaper clippings. This is because the products used within the albums were not acid- and lignin-free, terms my mother had never even heard of until recently. In this book you will learn why you should use archival-safe products and how scrapbooking has become a hobby enjoyed by millions of people around the world.

So, assemble your photos and get ready to create and discover innovative ideas and techniques that will enable you to relive those treasured memories created in your very own scrapbook.

The history of scrapbooking

The term 'scrapbook' was conceived because of the brightly coloured or decoratively cut remnants of paper, or scrap as it was sometimes called, that had been left over from the printers. People just loved to decorate their albums with these scrap pieces to add decoration and interest.

In 1826 John Poole published his book, *Manuscript Gleanings and Literary Scrapbook*. It showed the public how to display their mementoes, poems and scraps.

Ten years later in 1836, the first scrap album appeared which had an ornate cover, frames and divided title pages. Most scrapbook albums of the day contained postcards, sketches, calling cards and small embroidered pieces.

By the 1870s die-cuts and stamps were being made for decorative use in albums and, with the increasing popularity of the camera by the 1880s, the 'scrapbook' was revolutionised.

The author Mark Twain was such a devotee of the hobby of scrapbooking that he patented a series of scrapbooks in 1872. These albums contained gummed and non-gummed pages, with perforations to make them easy to remove. By 1901, over fifty-seven different types of his albums were available.

By the end of the First World War, the popularity of scrapbooking was on the decline, and by the Second World War it was almost non-existent.

Scrapbooking as we know it, evolved in the mid-1980s in the United States. At first, only albums, some basic tools and a few patterned papers and cardstock were available. As the hobby gained in popularity, more and more products became available and the scrapbook store was born. Scrapbooking is now one of the fastest growing hobbies in the world.

A scrapbook from the 1920s.

1. Getting organised

Getting organised

We have all been guilty at some time of rummaging through a box filled to the brim with photographs, looking for a certain photo you know is there. But, after sixty minutes of searching, you usually give up.

So how do you sort through the mess and begin putting your photos into a scrapbook album?

With a little organisation it will make scrapbooking so much easier and a lot less daunting.

To get started follow these easy steps:

Organise your photos into categories or themes, such as birthdays, holidays, Christmas, baby, toddler, school, pets, etc.

Using a photo-safe pen or pencil (never a ball point pen), write down any dates, names and memories you have onto the back of the photo or write onto a 'post-it' note. This will make journaling so much easier.

When you have finished sorting your photographs into themes, place them into chronological order.

Once you have done this, put all your photos into an acid-free photo box that has file tabs.

Store all of your negatives and photographs in acid- and lignin-free binders or boxes (which should also be PVC-free) and keep them in a dark, dry, cool environment.

Now you have organised your photographs, let's look at your work space.

Many people are lucky enough to have a spare room in their home to work from, which they can customise to suit their needs, whereas others have the dining room. I can remember my husband came home for many nights to a dining table strewn with photos, papers, equipment and more mess, to which his question would always be, 'I guess it's take-out tonight then?' It doesn't matter where you scrapbook or what space is available, you can still create beautiful pages and have lots of fun. If you don't have your own room, try customising a piece of furniture such as a wardrobe. Place shelves at the top for storing tools and die-cut machinery; use plastic boxes to store your punches, scissors, rubber stamp equipment and embellishments. If it has a heavy-duty shelf, that can act as your work surface, then when you have finished working on a layout, you simply close the doors and it will all be there waiting for you next time just how you left it.

30 x 30 cm (12" x 12") plastic storage boxes or carry cases are brilliant for keeping all your cardstock, paper and stickers neatly organised.

Jam jars and clear plastic containers are great for keeping together buttons, ribbons and odds and ends.

Tool boxes make an inexpensive solution for storing all those embellishments and small tools. Many of them have castors on so you can easily move them around.

There are many companies which specialise in scrapbook storage, whether it's modular or mobile.

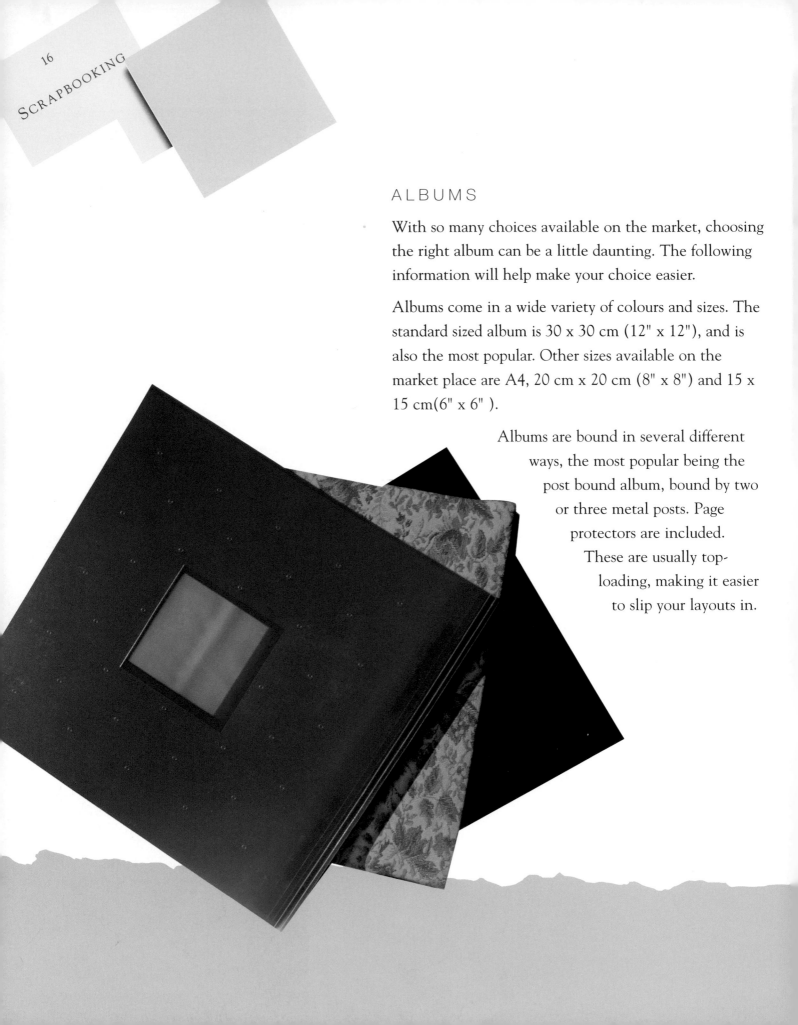

ALBUMS

With so many choices available on the market, choosing the right album can be a little daunting. The following information will help make your choice easier.

Albums come in a wide variety of colours and sizes. The standard sized album is 30 x 30 cm (12" x 12"), and is also the most popular. Other sizes available on the market place are A4, 20 cm x 20 cm (8" x 8") and 15 x 15 cm(6" x 6").

Albums are bound in several different ways, the most popular being the post bound album, bound by two or three metal posts. Page protectors are included. These are usually top-loading, making it easier to slip your layouts in.

The main advantage of this album is that its easy to change your page order around and to expand this album.

Simply add extension posts and more page protectors.

Ring binder albums, as the name suggests, are held together with two or three metal rings. The size of the ring determines the number of pages it will accommodate. It is very easy to change the order of your pages with this type of album.

Spiral-bound albums use a spiral wire to keep the covers and inside pages together. You can't add pages to these, but they do make great themed albums.

Strap-bound albums have a plastic strap which you hook your pages onto and allows the album to expand.

Whichever album style you decide on, make sure it is acid- and lignin-free as it will protect and store all your beautifully crafted pages.

Post bound Album

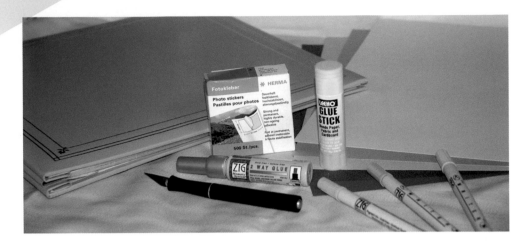

Basic tools

There are a few basic tools needed to begin scrapbooking, which are:

Photo-safe adhesives

Album

Acid- and lignin-free cardstock

Permanent and fade-resistant pen for journaling

Straight-edged scissors

Paper trimmer and/or guillotine

Other tools and embellishments you can add as you go along.

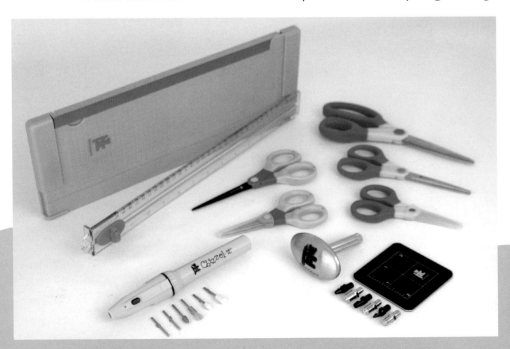

ADHESIVES

With so many types of adhesives, a newcomer to scrapbooking can be left wondering just where to start. The most important thing you need to know is that whatever adhesive you do choose, it must be acid-free (in Europe it is known as solvent-free). The reason for this is so that your photographs and work do not become damaged over time. You will also find that different adhesives work better on different surfaces.

DOUBLE-SIDED TAPE

This is available in various sized rolls and sheets. It works well for adhering cardstock and paper and is very useful for creating shaker boxes, making pockets and using glitters, micro beads and sand.

GLUE STICK

This works well on both cardstock and paper and it is easy to move items around while the glue is still wet, so it makes a good choice for covering items.

GLUE PEN

These contain wet glue and have a variety of tips, from a tiny ball point, to the jumbo size. When used wet, many of these glues have a permanent finish, but if you let them dry first before sticking down, they are removable. Use this glue for tiny embellishments, paper and vellum.

GLUE DOTS

These circles come in a wide array of sizes and thicknesses and are great for adhering metal, buttons and embellishments which have a bit of weight to them.

TAPE DISPENSER

These come in both permanent and repositionable tabs and mini dots varieties. Whichever you choose, they work well on photographs, papers, cardstock and embellishments.

PHOTO TABS

These come in a dispenser box and are double-sided stickers. As the name suggests, they are used for sticking down photographs, but are also useful with papers and cardstock.

XYRON

This is a brilliant machine that comes in different sizes and can turn just about anything into a sticker.

CARDSTOCK

Cardstock is the staple of all scrapbook albums. It comes in different sizes, weights, finishes and textures. You can buy it in single sheets or in multi packs, but do make sure it is acid- and lignin-free.

PATTERNED PAPER AND VELLUMS

Acid- and lignin-free patterned papers and vellums (semi-transparent paper) are available in endless colours, patterns and finishes. Use them for backgrounds, borders and matting your photographs.

Scissors and paper trimmer

A good pair of sharp, straight-edged scissors, with a fine point, and a trimmer or guillotine (that can take a 12" sheet of paper), is essential for any scrapbooker. These tools are the best means of cutting down and trimming cardstock, papers and photos. Decorative edged scissors are also available and can give a different look to any straight edge.

A craft knife allows you to cut intricate shapes accurately. You can also use one to position small stickers very precisely.

A cutting mat is essential when using a craft knife. The best ones are called 'self-healing' because the cut marks re-seal.

RULERS, TEMPLATES AND SHAPE CUTTERS

A metal ruler is vital for cutting straight lines with a craft knife. Use an acrylic ruler for measuring card and paper. Templates and shape cutters help you create your own die cuts, crop photos into fun shapes, or cut cardstock and paper into photo mats, frames and decorative borders.

PENS AND PENCILS

One of the most important parts of scrapbooking is to write something down, and this is known as journaling. There are a wide variety of coloured pens with different tips that can make any handwriting look decorative, but be sure it is pigment based and fade proof.

Photo-safe pencils can be used for adding shading and colour, or simply use them to write on the back of a photograph.

EMBELLISHMENTS

There is so much variety out there when it comes to embellishments, from tiny metal buckles to use with ribbon, to coloured safety pins and fabric or leather pockets. Listed below is a wide array of products available, but remember, whichever embellishments you choose to enhance your layouts with, try not to overwhelm the page with them.

THREADS AND WIRE

There are some fabulous ribbons, fibres, raffia, and threads that are great for attaching buttons, beads and charms. They also add that finishing touch to a tag and can be used as binding for a mini book.

Wires come in different colours and gauges. The higher the gauge, the thinner the wire. You can use wire the same way as the threads, but be sure to use wire cutters to ensure you don't damage your scissors.

STICKERS

Stickers come in thousands of designs. You can choose hand crafted stickers made from fabrics and other embellishments which are 3-D.

Many stickers come on rolls or in packaged sheets and you simply peel them off and apply where you want. You can choose from many different types of designs and themes, from the tooth fairy or beautiful scenery, to poems and words. Rub-down stickers are another option. These come in packaged sheets or small booklets of words, letters or designs. You simply transfer them using a lollipop stick.

METAL

There is such an array of metal embellishments, mini metal frames and slide mounts which add a wonderful dimension to a photo. They also add a lovely touch to the decoration of an album. Metal alphabet charms and tokens give a dramatic impact to any layout, as do hinges and washers. Brads and eyelets are one of the most versatile metal embellishments. They are available in a variety of different metal finishes, from antique to pewter, and in a fabulous range of fun colours. You can also buy these embellishments in different sizes and shapes, from a basic circle shape, to a heart, star, flower and more.

Brads are like a paper fastener with a split pin back. Simply push the brad through, or make a small hole if you are using several thicknesses of card and open out the back. They add dimension to a page and are useful for attaching vellums, acetate and other elements to your page. To attach an eyelet, you need an eyelet setting kit. There are several different kinds to choose from. The original kit consists of a hole punch, a setter, a setting mat and a hammer; other kits require no hammer.

Other embellishments include the ever popular buttons, which come in so many different colours, sizes and shapes and in a huge variety of themes.

Chalks and rub-on paints add depth to die-cuts, pages and torn edges of cardstock and paper. Try using chalks and pigment inks to age your paper. Try crumpling it first to achieve a more interesting effect. To apply chalks, rub-on paints and pigment inks, use the applicator they usually come with, or a make-up pad, cotton wool, sponge, or cotton bud.

Rubber stamps are available in so many designs and alphabets. When used on a layout with pigment inks or embossed, they can create a stunning, original look.

To emboss, simply press a rubber stamp into pigment ink or a clear inkpad. Apply the stamp to your cardstock or paper and shake your chosen colour of embossing powder over the image. Tap off any excess and heat the area using a heat gun.

Craft punches come in various sizes with a multitude of designs. Use them to create fun designs on your pages, or to dress up a tag or border.

Personal die-cutting machines are a wonderful addition for any crafter. They will enable you to cut alphabets and shapes out of cardstock and paper, as well as fabrics, thin metal sheets, foam and shrink plastic. You can really add your own unique look to your pages every time.

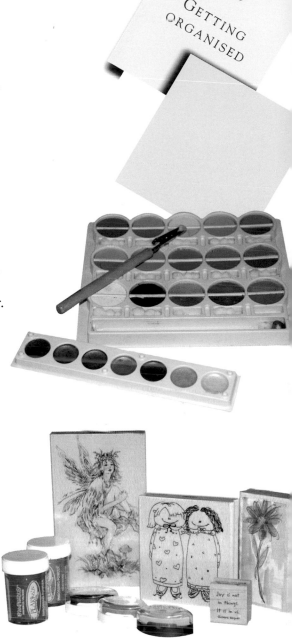

2. Basic techniques

You are now familiar with the history, terminology and the tools used in scrapbooking. Now it's time to create your very first layout.

You don't have to be unbelievably creative or a professional designer to make an appealing layout, just follow the simple techniques listed.

Photograph

Pictures and paper

When creating your page, it is important to have a main focal point. This is where your eye will usually look first. Select photos that convey what you want to say and that are good sharp images. Choose a single photo that will be your main focus, then pick other photos (these may be smaller or the same size images) to support your chosen theme. There are no rules as to how many photographs are allowed on a page. You can have a single photograph or a whole collection of them – the choice is yours.

Cropped photograph

Cropping your photos

Cropping your photographs can add emphasis and style to the image. When cropping, remember to cut away less than you think, as you can always take more off but you can't always put it back on. A good solution to this is to always have double prints made. If you only have a single copy, then scan the image into your computer and make several copies. You don't just have to crop your photos with straight edges, try using a template to create fun shapes.

Choosing cardstock and paper

Cardstock and patterned papers are always at the forefront of all your layouts. An easy way to choose colours for your page, is to pick colours from your photos, or choose something that contrasts with it. Colour does set the mood for your layout, so try to pick colours that support the photo, not compete with it.

Matting

Matting your photographs brings emphasis to them, and makes them stand out. To mat a photo, cut your cardstock or paper to a larger size than your photo, then adhere your picture on top. You can mat your photos once or as many times as you wish. For a different look to your mat, try tearing the edges or use a shaped template.

Putting it together

Once you have chosen your background papers and photographs, you need to arrange your layout. Before you stick anything down, try moving your photos around the page until you feel you have the balance right. Once you are happy with how it looks, you can start adding your chosen embellishments.

The finished layout

Journaling

No layout is complete without some journaling. We've all heard the old saying 'a picture is worth a thousand words', but sometimes the story in the picture needs to be told.

Many people find that journaling is the hardest part of their scrapbooking, but it is also one of the most important. You take a photograph to capture a moment in time that means something to you. By adding the journaling, you convey the story behind it; after all, it's the story that makes your scrapbook album so unique and special.

At the very least, your journaling should include names, dates, and places; for layouts with children, include their ages.

To expand on your basic journaling, try adding poems and quotes about the subject. There are plenty of books and websites containing wonderful sayings. Alternatively, use an actual saying or song that was a favourite of whoever you are creating the layout for.

If you are stuck for what to write about, here are a few points to consider.

Ask family members about their favourite things, such as memories, school, holidays, food, friends or birthdays.

Record how each child has grown, every year on their birthday, not only in height but in what they have achieved.

Write about your home, what you like about it, what you are hoping to change. Who are your neighbours?

What about your family traditions, how did they start, do you keep adding new ones?

Record all those funny moments, whether it's a comment from one of your children or the camping trip where you forgot to bring the sleeping bags!

When journaling, try to use your own handwriting occasionally as it's part of you. On the next page are a few simple ways to change the look of your own handwriting.

Top tip

Always write on a piece of card, paper, tag or die-cut – if you make a mistake you can simply create another. If you journal directly onto the page and make a mistake, it's a lot harder to rectify.

Christmas light
writing

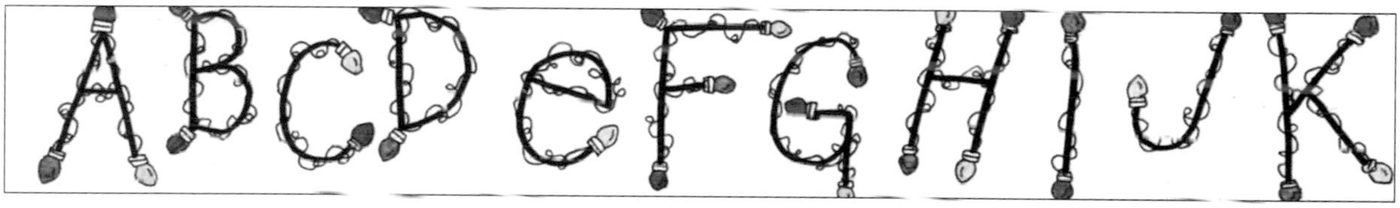

ABCDEFGHIJK

Dot writing

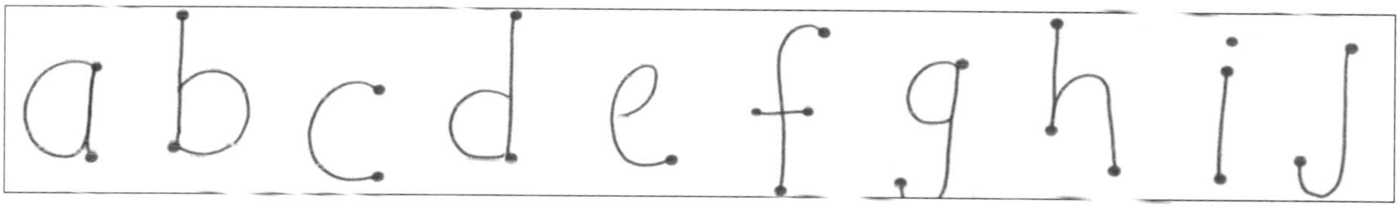

abcdefghij

Curly writing

ABCDEFGHjK

Heart writing

abcdefghl

Floral writing

ABCDeFG

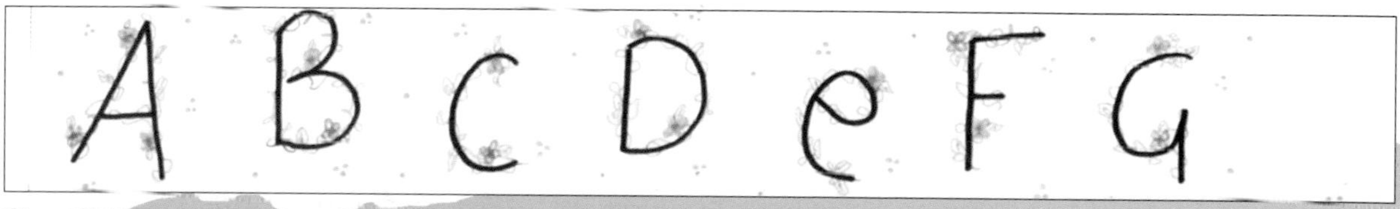

THE COLOUR WHEEL

We are all surrounded by colour, which often influences our moods – a bright sunny day lifts our spirits and makes us happy, whereas a dark and overcast day can make us feel sad.

When choosing the colours for your layouts, remember you are setting the scene for your photos: soft pastels or brights; bold and funky or strong and sophisticated.

Choosing colours for a layout can be a little daunting, which is why a colour wheel can come in useful. It helps you understand how colours can relate to each other. It can also take a lot of the guesswork out of which colour schemes will work.

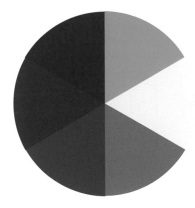

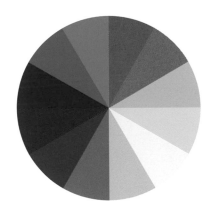

PRIMARY COLOURS
Red, yellow and blue

Primary colours are the three basic colours, they can not be mixed from any other colours

SECONDARY COLOURS
Green, orange and purple

These are the results obtained by mixing the primary colours. For example, if you mix blue and yellow you get green; red and yellow make orange, and blue and red make purple.

TERTIARY COLOURS
Red and orange, yellow and orange, yellow and green, blue and green, blue and purple and red and purple.

These are the colour results obtained by mixing a primary colour with a secondary colour. For example, if you mix yellow and green together you achieve lime green which is a tertiary colour.

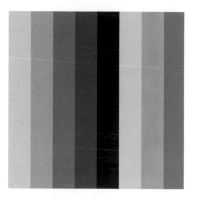

NEUTRAL COLOURS
WHITE, GREY, BLACK AND BEIGE

Neutral colours will go with any colour on the wheel, and sometimes neutral colours can have a slight hint of another colour, such as white mixed with yellow, but if you mix yellow with black you have created a shade.

COOL COLOURS

WARM COLOURS

Now you understand how colours relate to each other on the colour wheel, here are a few more tips.

Colours fall into two categories, either cool or warm. Blues and greens are usually known as cool, and reds and yellows are warm colours.

Mixing shades of cool and warm colours together isn't a problem, but just make sure you pay attention to the balance. If you find creating a colour scheme a little daunting, try to use colours that are the same hue. For example, if you are using a pastel pink, find the same colour value in a blue or yellow. If you want to use a deep red, again, look on the colour wheel and find the same strength of colour only in a completely different shade. Remember you are using colour to enhance your photographs, so try using it just as an accent.

1

The following categories explain the different types of colour schemes you can create:

1. *Analogous.* This colour scheme uses between two and four colours which are next to each other on the colour wheel. These colours work well together because of their corresponding undertones.

2. *Complementary.* These colours are exact opposites on the colour wheel.

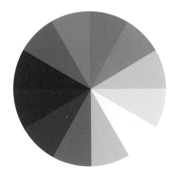

2

3

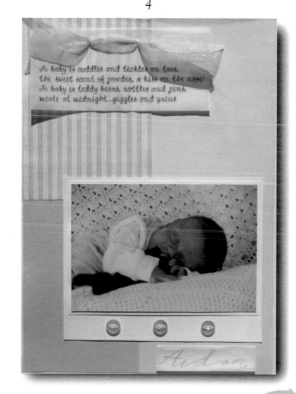

4

3. Monochromatic. When using these colours you can create many different looks by simply using a variety of different shades of a single colour.

4. Triadic. This colour scheme uses three colours from the colour wheel that are equally distanced from one another. Using a triadic colour scheme creates a high-contrast look to your layout, as the three colours chosen will be very different. Yet, when used together in just the right balance, you will have a great looking layout.

3. Photography

Photography

I love taking photographs, in fact, if there was an award for being snap happy with a camera, then I'd win. I carry a camera with me at all times, and always keep one in the car. I even use the camera on my phone, because you just never know when that perfect photo opportunity might arise. My husband despairs and reckons that I'm worse than any tourist. My children all groan when they see the camera being taken out. Hopefully, when they're ninety, they will appreciate all the photographs and remember all the wonderful, sad, crazy and fun moments of growing up.

As all scrapbookers know, when creating a scrapbook album, one of the most important parts will be your photographs. These are the memories you have chosen to capture on film to preserve for generations to come.

Cameras come in a variety of models: digital, point-and-shoot, and the SLR models with changeable lenses. Whichever camera you own, there are always ways to get a better photograph. The following tips and techniques will help you capture better pictures more effectively, and become a more accomplished photographer.

Make sure your subject is in sharp focus.

Composition

What makes a good photograph? Is it picking up your camera, taking aim at the subject, pressing the button and hoping for the best? Read through these tips and take a little time when taking your shots and you'll find yourself taking better photos.

FILL THE FRAME

When you look through the viewfinder of your camera, you don't always see what's going on. You might not notice slight distractions such as a tree branch growing out of someone's head, or you might misjudge the actual distance and end up with lots of wasted space around the subject. The easiest way to remedy this is to move in a little closer to your subject and, before you actually press the shutter, look around your view finder. Is there too much space, or an object that looks like it could be growing from your composition? With a little extra thought, you can produce well-composed pictures.

THE RULE OF THIRDS

This is probably the best known rule in photography. The principle is that an imaginary line divides the image into thirds, both vertically and horizontally. You would place what you feel is the more important element of your composition where the lines intersect.

Not only can you use the intersections, you can place areas of the composition into strips using a third. By using the rule of thirds you will create an instantly balanced and pleasing picture.

Photograph using natural light

Lighting

When taking your photographs, one of the best forms of lighting is natural light, and the best natural lighting is usually in the early morning and late afternoon. Direct sunlight produces harsh shadows and brilliant highlights, strong colours are more intense and weaker colours are more washed out. Diffused sunlight can be caused by haze and mist in the air. It produces soft shadows and flat highlights, making colours that are saturated and vibrant.

Using a flash or fill-in flash helps to even-out shadows caused by the sun. For instance, when you take a close up photo of a person in sunlight, one side of the face will be in shadow – using the fill-in flash helps to eliminate this.

Top tip

When taking photographs outside, DO NOT shoot into the sun.

Taking portraits

Here are a few tips to help you improve on your own portrait photos:

- Use a camera that has a zoom lens, so you can get in close.

- You need a good light source. Try natural light – indirect window light works well for this – or else use flash lighting.

- Use a backdrop such as a plainly painted wall. If you only have wallpapered walls, put up a white or black sheet.

- Crop the subject whilst still in the frame.

- Use a higher film speed. The higher the number the more sensitive it is, consequently it needs less light. Use 400 ASA/ISO or above.

- Shoot from different angles. Get close and pose your subjects. Use props: they don't have to be fancy, even a chair will do. If you are using more than one person, shoot in close-up and have their heads at different levels.

- Take plenty of shots.

- Experiment with black and white film.

Digital cameras

There is definitely something to be said about 'going digital'. I only acquired a digital camera at the beginning of this year, so I am still learning, but I'm already seeing the advantages.

Buy a large memory card – 256mb or bigger – so that you can take lots of pictures. I can get over 140 shots with my camera and I love seeing the images immediately and having the ability to keep taking the shots over and over until I am happy.

When you have a digital camera you don't always have to play it safe by keeping it in automatic mode. You can immediately see the results and experiment with the different settings. Using a digital camera also allows you to experiment with computer software editing programmes such as Photoshop and Paint Shop Pro.

Digital imaging using –software example

Top tip

Whatever your camera, keep it clean. Remove dust from the lens using a microfibre cloth or a photographic blower brush. These work well on the LCD screen of a digital camera too. There is always the huff method where you breathe onto the lens and gently wipe it with a soft, dry cloth. You can also use a soft dry cloth to keep the body of your camera clean. Never use a detergent or solvent-based cleaner. Replace your batteries as needed (or keep them charged).

Top tip

Keep a spare roll of film and battery in your camera bag – you never know when you might need them.

Here are a few tips to ensure that the photos you are taking of an event or place always come out right.

- Some scrapbookers have been known to take a photograph of their children wearing a certain colour so that it will work with a particular paper pattern they have.

- Why are you here at this particular event? Is it a friend's wedding? Are you on a picnic with the children? Are you on the holiday of a lifetime, or are you watching the FA cup final? With this in mind, what kind of photos will best describe what you are seeing?

- Try to get a photo of your surroundings. If you are on that holiday of a lifetime, you might never visit that place again. Or is it your very first Christmas as a married couple? Take a photo of your Christmas tree.

These events will become your memories. What will you want to remember about them?

things I love about you

Megan, you had so much fun at the Tamar Valley Donkey Park

4.Step-by-step

STEP-BY-STEP

Have you ever seen a page layout and wondered how they achieved that look? Or, have you picked up a tool, then hastily put it straight down because you didn't know how it worked? This section of the book will cover the basic 'how to' of scrapbooking.

Cropping your photographs

A photo is taken to capture a memory and freeze it in time. The thought of then taking a pair of scissors, craft knife, or a paper trimmer to cut it, can be a little intimidating. Don't be scared: cropping your photographs can actually improve them.

Before you start to crop a photograph, take a good look at the focal point and decide how much you need to crop to create better focus. Do you really need to keep those strangers in the picture? By cropping them out you will enhance the photo. A great way to make a decision, is to lay pieces of card over the areas you are thinking of cropping away. When you do crop the photo, always take less than you think. Remember, you can always take more off, but you can't put it back on!

When looking at a photo you are thinking of cropping, here a few things to keep in mind:

■ Are there empty spaces or shadows in the photo?

■ Are there people who you do not know, or maybe there is an arm or a leg that has made its way onto your photograph?

■ Is part of the photo out of focus?

■ When it comes to images and backgrounds such as buildings, houses, cars and transportation, you may want to keep them in the photograph as they might have sentimental importance in years to come. If you are undecided about a photograph, make a duplicate to crop and keep the original in one piece.

Use the following to crop photos:

■ Scissors

■ Ruler and pencil

■ Paper trimmer

■ Shaped stencils or personal die-cutter

Matting your photographs

Your photos are one of the most important parts of your layout and what better way to highlight them, than to mat them. To make a mat, you choose cardstock and/or patterned paper that will complement the colours in the photograph. An easy way to do this, is to place the photo onto different colours. You are looking for colours that complement, not detract from the photo.

ONCE YOU HAVE DECIDED ON YOUR PAPERS, FOLLOW THESE EASY STEPS:

1 Place your photo into the corner of your chosen card or paper, leaving the desired width around the two pre-cut sides

2 Measure the width you have chosen and place a mark using a pencil.

3 Cut the remaining two sides using a paper trimmer and mount your photo on top

You can mat your photos as many times as you wish. For a different look, try tearing the edges of the card or paper. The easiest way to do this, is to cut the card or paper approximately half an inch larger all the way around. You could even alternate the mat from straight-edged to torn-edged, or even use fancy-edged scissors.

How to use a craft knife

Have you ever looked at some of the intricately cut details on a card or scrapbook page and wondered how it was done?

The answer is simple: they used a craft knife. This tool is easy to use and always gives a clean cut. To ensure you always get a crisp clean cut, regularly change the blade in your knife.

When cutting a straight edge use a metal ruler as your guide and hold the craft knife against the edge of the ruler.

Use a brass or plastic template when cutting out shapes as it is easier to work with a guide.

When cutting out shapes freehand, try using blue tack to keep your card or paper in place.

Always have a self-healing mat under your card or paper to prevent damage to your work surface.

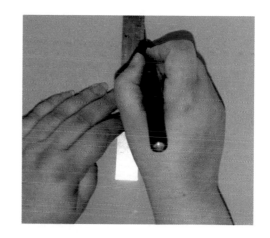

You can cut some amazing titles and letters using a craft knife. Use a standard word-processing programme on your computer to choose your font and the size. Then click on the bold button which will enlarge the shape and make it easier to cut. Print it in reverse (backwards) on the backside of your paper. It is easier to start by cutting out the middle of your letters, then continue by cutting around the edges.

Tearing paper

You can sometimes look at a layout or a photo mat and know it's not working for you. An easy way to change the look of your work, is to quite simply tear the cardstock or paper; it gives a softer look and is easy to do.

Cut your paper to size leaving an additional half an inch to the side you wish to tear, or leave it all the way around if you are going to tear all four sides.

If you are right-handed, hold the paper in your left hand and use your right hand to tear the paper using your fingers as a guide and to keep control. If you are left-handed, do exactly the same only with opposite hands.

For a unique look, use coloured paper with a white background. This way the tear will be white. You can leave it like this or add chalk or pigment inks along the torn edge to change the colour.

Tearing doesn't have to be for straight edges – you can also use a template to create fun shapes.

Top tip

Use torn strips of card and paper

to create borders.

Using chalk

Chalk is a great way of adding interest to your layouts. You can use it to add highlights and shadows to die-cuts, vellums, torn edges, dry embossed images and punched out shapes. You can even create your own unique background papers using chalks.

You can use several different applicators for different effects, but whichever one you choose, make sure you use a circular motion.

Using an eye-shadow applicator will give a rich colour as it holds a lot of chalk. A cotton bud works best on small areas and gives a softer, lighter finish. A make-up sponge or cotton pad is great for larger areas, such as making your own backgrounds. Try blending other colours as well.

Top tip

If you are worried about the chalk rubbing off, use hairspray to fix it.

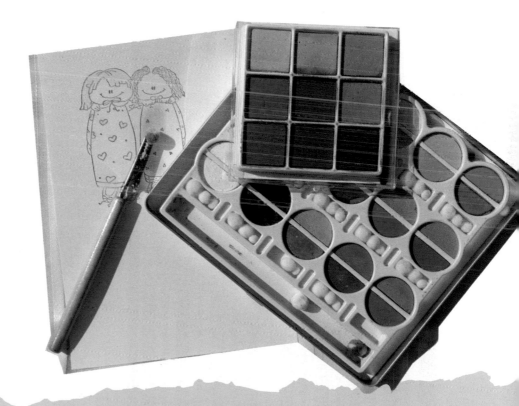

How to emboss

Dry embossing is a fun and easy technique to add interest and dimension to many projects.

All you need is a template which are available in brass or plastic in hundreds of designs.

A stylus, which is a tool that has a smooth round ball on either end, can be used for gently rubbing the outline of the template to reveal the raised edge. Low-tack masking tape helps keep the template and paper in place, and a light box or a window with lots of light makes it much easier to see the shape you are wanting to emboss.

Top tip

Embossing isn't only for card and paper – use vellum instead.

How to set an eyelet

Eyelets are a popular scrapbooking embellishment. They come in a wide array of colours, shapes, and even alphabets.

You don't just have to use an eyelet to finish off a tag. Use them as accents on die-cuts, or as the centre of a punched-out flower. Use them to attach other embellishments onto your page, such as vellum, fabric and fibres.

There are several different tools on the market you can choose to set an eyelet. The basic tool is an anywhere hole punch, an eyelet setter, a self-healing mat and a hammer.

FOLLOW THESE INSTRUCTIONS:

1   Place the card over the self-healing mat and make a hole where desired using an anywhere hole punch and hammer.

2   Put the eyelet through the hole and turn the card over. Take an eyelet setter and place it into the back of the eyelet, then gently tap the end using a hammer until the back of the eyelet has become flat.

3   You can then remove the eyelet setter and flatten the back further if required using the hammer.

4   There are also silent eyelet setters available on the market which don't require hammers.

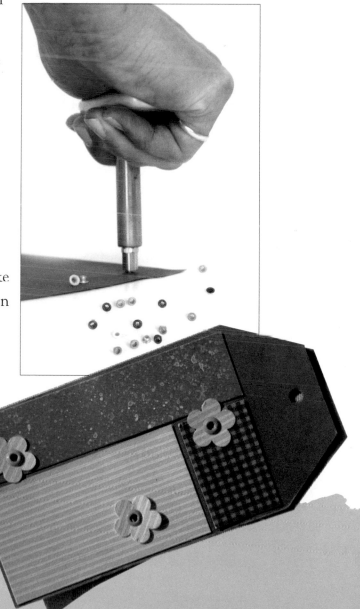

How to use fibres

Fibres and ribbons can add an elegant or funky look to any layout, and they are available in all sorts of styles, textures and widths.

You can use then as accents for tags, to bind mini books, even wrap them around a photo, or use them as a border.

To attach the fibre, you can use glue dots or double sided tape.

Thread your fibre through eyelets, or just weave the fibre through the holes created before setting the eyelet.

Place brads at the points desired and wrap the fibre around them, or put the fibre between the points of the brad before you push it through the card or paper.

Top tip

Create fun borders weaving your fibres through brads or eyelets that create the look of a corset.

Using die-cuts

Die-cut shapes are made by placing paper, card or even fabric over a die shape that goes through a machine. There are literally hundreds of shapes and alphabets to choose from. When you are looking for that extra special embellishment that is unique for your page, die-cuts are a great option. You can mat them, layer them, stamp and emboss them, highlight them with chalks, accent them with metal embellishments, even take a sewing machine and stitch them.

Choose the machine that best suits your needs and start having fun cutting and even embossing.

PHOTO

TITLE

5. Planning your pages

PLANNING YOUR PAGES

Most of you reading this book will at some time have taken a journey by car or on foot using a map. You plan your chosen route carefully to ensure you see points of interest along the way and if you follow the directions, you will always reach your destination without any difficulty. But, if you choose a different road, it might take you a little longer, but you will see different places and as long as you keep referring to your map, you will still eventually make it to your destination. Using a sketch is like having a map: you know what the end result is going to be, but if you make a few changes, it will still be similar just more unique to you. Sketches are definitely a simple way to create easy, inspired work every time.

I have over one hundred sketches that I keep safe in a file folder that I can refer to whenever I get 'scrapper's block'. No two layouts ever look the same because you will use different photos, colours and embellishments and the sketches are time-saving, too.

To draw a sketch you don't have to be an artist, or even be able to draw a straight line. I make my sketches using blank sheets of A4 card. I then use a pencil to do my initial work and when I am happy with the results, I go over the lines with a black marker and store it in a ring binder, with notes about the papers, stickers and card used.

You can choose whatever works for you – a blank book, lined paper, pens, pencils or crayons. The more you do it, the easier it becomes.

TIP: Take your inspiration from books, magazines, clothing, CD covers, whatever attracts your eye.

Chloe

SUPPLIES

Cardstock: Bazzil

Pattern Paper: Daisy D, Bo Bunny,

Cloud 9, Karen Foster.

Stickers: Making Memories

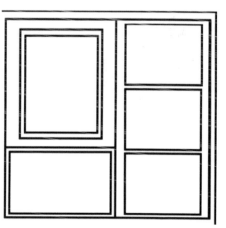

Mummy's favourite walk

SUPPLIES

Pattern paper and card: Arctic Frog

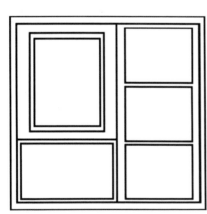

Live today

SUPPLIES

Pattern paper and cardstock: Bo
Bunny Press
Stickers: Bo Bunny Press

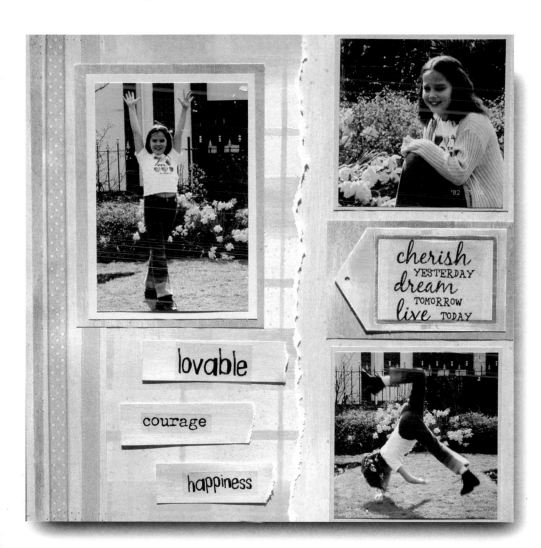

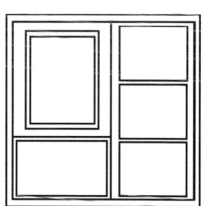

Megan

SUPPLIES

Pattern paper: Daisy D

Embellishments: Making Memories, Stationery Box, Daisy D

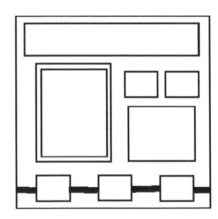

Friends

SUPPLIES

Cardstock: PTC Company

Pattern paper: Bo Bunny Press

Stickers: Bo Bunny Press

Pen: Zig writer

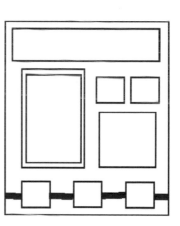

Brother

SUPPLIES
Cardstock: Bazzil
Pattern paper: Daisy D
Stickers: Bo Bunny
Embellishments: Making Memories

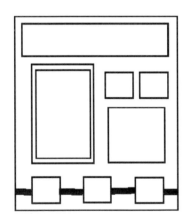

I hope you dance

SUPPLIES

Cardstock: Craft work cards

Pattern paper: Bo Bunny

Stickers: Bo Bunny

Rub ons: Making memories

Tags: My Mind's Eye

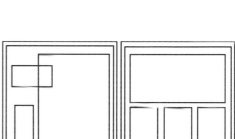

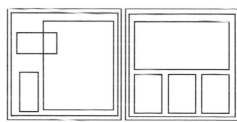

Y.W. Camp

SUPPLIES

Cardstock: PTC Company

Pattern paper: Cloud 9

Stickers: Bo Bunny Press

Sea Zoo

SUPPLIES
Cardstock: PTC Company
Pattern paper: Daisy D, Bo bunny
Stickers: Making Memories

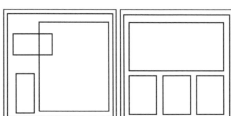

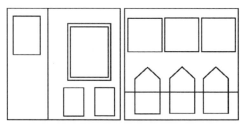

Fun

SUPPLIES
Cardstock: Bazzil
Pattern paper: Vellum, Buttons
Stickers: S.E.I.

Top tip

*Use the negative of your alphabet sticker to create
a fun title, by placing it over cropped photo waste.*

Merry Christmas

SUPPLIES

Cardstock: Bazzil

Pattern paper: Daisy D

Buttons and ribbon: unknown

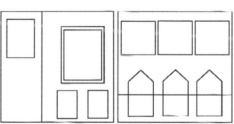

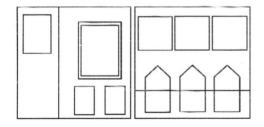

Happy Birthday

SUPPLIES

Cardstock: S.E.I.

Pattern paper: S.E.I., Bo Bunny

Stickers: Bo Bunny

Ribbon: unknown

Dylan

SUPPLIES

Cardstock: Bo Bunny

Pattern paper: Karen Foster, Daisy D

Embellishments: Making Memories, Jolees Boutique

Alphabet stickers: Arctic Frog

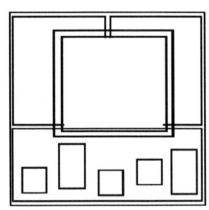

The Gibson Family

SUPPLIES

Cardstock: PTC Company

Pattern paper: Daisy D

Font: Rage italic

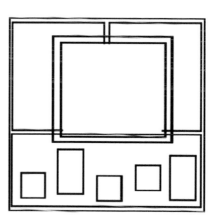

Sun, sand, sea

SUPPLIES

Cardstock: PTC company

Pattern paper and stickers: Bo Bunny Press

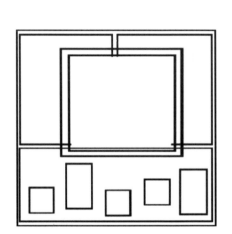

Joseph and his Technicolour Dreamcoat

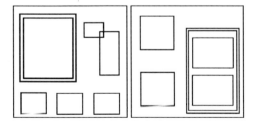

SUPPLIES

Cardstock: The PTC company

Patterned paper: Sweet Water, Daisy D, Bo Bunny Press

Stickers: Arctic Frog

Rub ons: Making Memories

My sister, my friend

SUPPLIES

Cardstock: The PTC company

Patterned paper: Sweet Water, Bo Bunny

Stickers: Bo Bunny

Embellishments: Making Memories

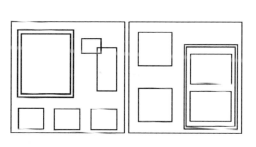

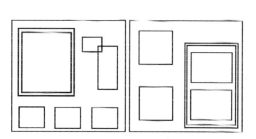

Experience, Discover, Adventure

SUPPLIES

Cardstock: Bo Bunny

Stickers: Arctic Frog

Sketches

Here are a collection of sketches for you to refer to.
See what you can do with them.

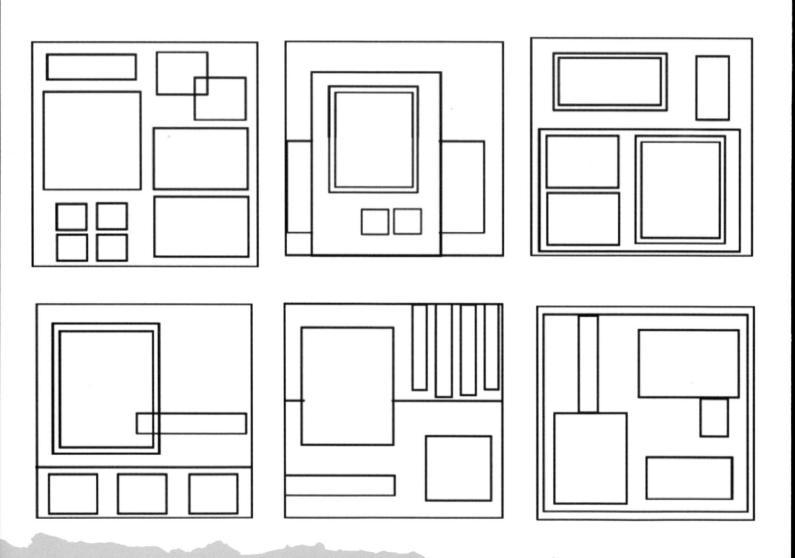

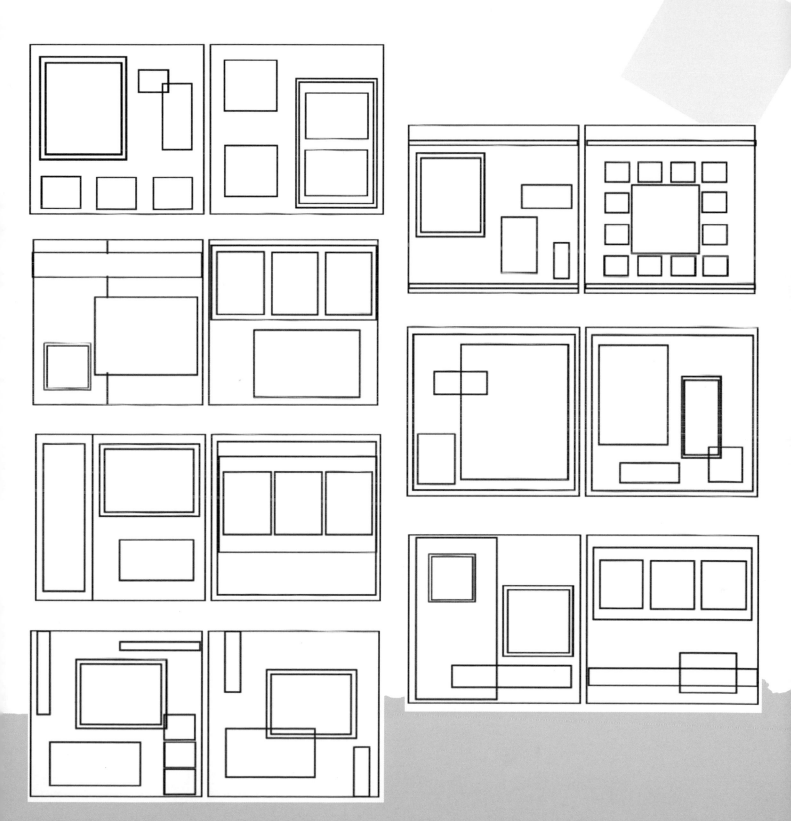

6. Projects

CREATING A MINI ALBUM

MATERIALS NEEDED

Cardstock in creams, white, deep red and evergreen

Cream vellum

Patterned papers to complement cardstock and photographs (I used Daisy D papers)

Red metal-rimmed tags

A good selection of ribbons, lace and twill

Alphabet, poem and word stickers

Peel-offs

Brads and nail heads

Funky paper clips

A kit or cut chosen cardstock to measure 5" x 6.5"

TOOLS NEEDED

Paper trimmer

Hole punch

Staples

When you are new to scrapbooking, creating a twenty-, forty-, or even a sixty-paged album can seem a little daunting. A mini album can be a great way to start your scrapbooking journey. Because they are small, giving them a theme such as love, family, wedding, a birthday, and so on, works really well. They make lovely gifts and are the perfect size to carry with you in a handbag; you can usually make the entire album in a day. Mini albums can be bought in kits or you can create your own to the size you wish.

The mini album I've created here has a family theme and has photographs of my husband and me, and my children at different ages. I keep it close by and often pull it out just to remember how blessed I am with having such a beautiful family.

To cover the front of your mini album, choose your photo and mat it with a complementary colour. Place two gold peel-off corner stickers onto opposite corners of the photo, then adhere it to the front cover of the album. Using alphabet stickers, put the word 'memories' on top.

1   For your first page, place a word sticker onto a metal-rimmed tag, then tie a bow. Cut a piece of patterned paper approximately 9 x 13 cm (3½" x 5¼") and adhere it down. Cut one thin strip of patterned paper 3 x 14.5 cm (1¼" x 5¾"), and one thick strip of card 5 x 14. 5 cm (2" x 5¾"), and stick them together, to create a border. Using your hole punch, put three holes along the top left side and thread assorted ribbons through, tying the ends. Stick the border down, gluing only three sides so you can use it as a pocket, then adhere the tag. Repeat this for the inside back cover.

Steps 1 and 2.

2   Tear a small square approximately 7.5 x 7.5 cm (3" x 3") and mat it to your chosen cardstock. Place a poem sticker on top. Cut a piece of patterned paper 10 x 14 cm (4" x 5½") and adhere it down, embellish with two gold corner peel-offs. To this adhere your matted poem, place a piece of organza ribbon on top, then gently push through three nail heads to hold it in place and add decoration. Cut a small piece of lace, fold it in half and place it on the tab or edge of the bottom right side, hold in place with a brad.

Steps 3 and 4.

3 Cut a piece of patterned paper to the size required, then crop your photo and stick it down. Stick a piece of organza ribbon with glue dots and embellish it with sticker words and a funky paper clip.

4 Cut a piece of card to 7.5 x 10 cm (3" x 4") and embellish it with patterned paper, a metal tag that has been threaded with ribbon and decorated, and a piece of lace held down by staples. Adhere it using double-sided tape on three sides, so you have created a pocket to place a photo in. Along the tab or right side, place three brads or nail heads.

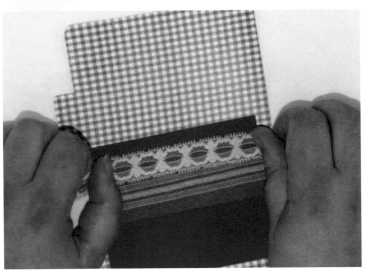

Step 4

Steps 5 & 6

Steps 7 and 8

5 Make a small border for the left side of the page using cardstock and patterned paper. Tear a piece of vellum on both sides and stick on top. Place your photo beneath and add a sticker or create your own using a dymo labeller.

6 Cut strips of ribbon in various lengths and staple them to your page so that they all criss cross one another. Place embellishments or photos between the ribbon. Along the tab or the right side, place a word sticker.

7 Wrap a piece of ribbon around the bottom of a 8 x 13 cm (3¼" x 5") piece of patterned paper and stick both of the ends to the back. Tie a metal-rimmed tag to the ribbon. Mat your chosen photo and stick it down off-centre.

Step 8

8 Out of your chosen patterned paper, cut two different sized rectangles. One will be 13 x 9 cm (5" x 3½"), the other 6 x 9.5 cm (2¼" x 3¾"), and adhere them to the page overlapping one another. Mat your photograph and create a phrase using a dymo labeller or sticker words. Fold a piece of ribbon in half and staple it to the tab, or at the top of the right side.

9 Create a border by cutting a strip of patterned paper. Adhere this to the left side of your page. Measure a 7..5 cm (3") square out of vellum to make an envelope. You do this by marking the middle of the square, then fold in three corners so that they slightly overlap one another. Stick them down using a glue pen. Adhere a printed piece of twill on top and place a photo within the envelope. Add an embellishment of your choice.

Step 9

You can bind the mini album together in several different ways. I chose to put two holes through all twelve pages using a hole punch and tied it together with organza ribbon.

CREATING A HERITAGE PAGE

We all have photos that date from early in the 20th century. Most are black and white, others are sepia and a few have been hand-tinted.

I love looking through my family's old photos. I wonder what it was like to live back then. Did they ever think that someone fifty, sixty, or even a hundred years on would be looking at their photographs? When I look at photos of my grandmother as a child in the 1920s, I can see my daughter, who looks just like her. She is also just as strong-willed!

When working with your heritage photos, never cut the original. If you want to crop it, make a duplicate and crop that. Making a duplicate allows you to play. My grand-dad is eighty three and loves to reminisce with me. I often ask him questions about when he was small, and what his parents and grandparents were like, and believe me, he tells some wonderful stories. It's so important to record these things, even seemingly insignificant things like hair colour, for instance. I have only ever known my grand-dad with white hair, so being nosy, I asked him about it. With a duplicate photograph of him as a boy, and using coloured pens that are available just for this, I was able to tint it and make his hair colour blonde. It totally changed the photo.

This heritage layout has a collage feel to it. It looks like it has many layers but it doesn't. By using patterned papers and printed die-cuts that have printed lace, buttons and layers, you can easily and quickly create a layout that looks as though you have spent hours on it.

Top tip

Ask older family members if they can remember who the people in the photo are and where and when it was taken. You may even get some great stories about those people to use in your album.

Top tip

If the photograph is on a written postcard, scan the written side in and incorporate it onto your layout.

MATERIALS NEEDED

Brown cardstock

An assortment of printed vintage-look papers

Cream vellum

Funky paperclips

White metal-rimmed tags

Assorted old buttons

Pre-printed tags

TOOLS NEEDED

Paper trimmer

Chalks

Hole punch

Needle and thread

Trimming paper

Top tip

If you have a printed button on your paper or embellishment, stitch through it, or adhere or stitch an actual button nearby, it will make it look more 3D.

1 Take a sheet of 30 x 30 cm (12" x 12") printed floral paper and cut .½" off the top and right side. Tear approximately a quarter of the paper off. When tearing, pull the small piece towards you. This will leave you with a nice white tear along the large section left. Adhere this to the brown cardstock leaving a ¼" border around three sides.

2 Cut a 4 x 28 cm (1¼" x 11½") strip of music paper and age it by rubbing dark brown chalk on it in a circular motion, then mount it to the top of your layout leaving a small border.

3 Cut a 13 x 17 cm (5" x 6½") piece from the remaining music paper, and tear one side off. Mount this to the right of a strip of brown card measuring 5½" x 8⅛" and adhere this to the centre of the layout.

4 Cut a 14 x 19 cm (3½"x 7½") strip of cream vellum tearing a piece off the bottom on an angle and adhere to the left of the page so that it partially covers the music paper.

5 Cut a strip of lace print paper measuring 7 x 23 cm (2¾" x 9") and mount it to the bottom right of the page. Stitch through four different sized buttons and mount them on top using double-sided tape.

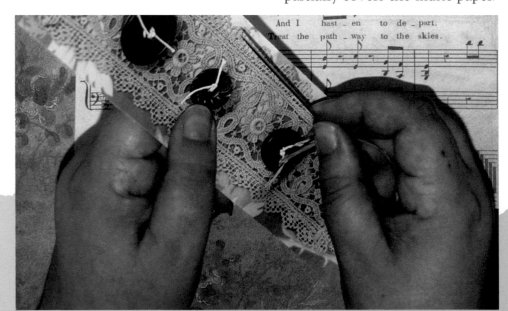

Stitching through buttons

6 Make two tags using papers and card left over. One should measure 6 x 12 cm (2½" x 4¾") and the other 2.5 x 5 cm (1" x 2"). Punch a hole through the top and place a funky clip through the smallest tag and hang it from the top left music strip. Mount the larger tag along the right edge. You could also use pre-printed tags.

7 Mount your photograph off-centre and journal on a strip of vellum. Place this over the bottom of the photo using funky paperclips.

8 Take a metal-rimmed tag and age it using chalks, journal on it and put a funky clip through. Place a couple of buttons wherever you wish and add some more journaling onto the vellum.

Ageing the tag.

Top tip

Try aging your paper by brushing a strong tea solution over it, or crumple the paper first and rub dark coloured chalks into the creases.

USING TRANSPARENCIES

Transparencies (transparent film) are a popular embellishment for scrapbookers. You can purchase them pre printed or clear, ready for you to print.

Because they are clear, transparencies are an excellent choice for journaling as it allows the photograph or patterned paper behind, to show through clearly, something vellum doesn't do.

When printing your own transparency sheets, print on the grainy side and change your computer setting to transparency. For added interest, print in colour or highlight the reverse side or just a few individual words using acrylic paint. To attach a transparency, you can use several different methods such as brads, eyelets, double-sided tape, staples, or you can even sew them on.

The following two page layouts have been created using 30 x 30 cm (12" x 12") transparency sheets. The first layout uses the entire sheet for embellishment, the second uses cut up pieces.

MATERIALS NEEDED:
Navy and pastel blue cardstock 30 x 30 cm (12" x 12")

Assorted patterned papers in blues and greens 30 x 30 cm (12" x 12")

Printed transparency 30 x 30 cm (12" x 12")

TOOLS NEEDED:
Paper trimmer

Double-sided tape

Top tip

Use your rubber stamps on transparencies.

Trimming paper

When creating a layout using a 30 x 30 cm (12" x 12") transparency you need to keep the layout very simple and place the photos where the print will cover part of them and the blank area covers the remainder of the photo.

1 Cut two strips of complementing patterned paper, one will measure 13 x 30 cm (5¼" x 12"), the other 16.5 x 30 (6½" x 12"). Mount them to the navy cardstock leaving a gap in the middle.

2 Out of green patterned paper, trim a square to measure 22 x 22 cm (8½" x 8½") and mat this to pastel blue card, then mount to the bottom right side of the page, right to the edge.

3 Crop two photographs and mat them both with navy cardstock. Mount them to the layout so that one slightly overlaps the other.

4 Journal on some left-over cardstock. You can mat this if you wish.

5 Take your transparency and mount it using double-sided tape, brads or eyelets.

Matting photo onto cardstock

MATERIALS NEEDED:

Cardstock in navy, beige and denim blue 30 x 30 cm (12" x 12")

Patterned paper in a large plaid, green and yellow 30 x 30 cm (12" x 12")

Transparency 30 x 30 cm (12" x 12")

Copper mini brads

Sepia-coloured pigment ink

TOOLS NEEDED

Paper trimmer

Corner rounder punch

Alphabet rubber stamps

1   Cut a strip of beige card 14..5 x 30 cm (5¾" x 11¾") and adhere to the bottom of the first page leaving a small border. Cut a second strip measuring 14..5 x 27 cm (5¾" x 10¾") and mount it to the top left half of the second page leaving a small border. Cut the large plaid-patterned paper in half and adhere one half to the top of the first page leaving a very small border, then duplicate this for the second page, only adhere it to the bottom half.

2   Using your alphabet stamps and ink stamp words to go with your photos, trim them into strips then take the ink pad and ink around all four sides – this gives them a matted look.

3   Take the transparency and cut it into desired sized strips. Place one strip along the top left hand side of the first page. Over this, mount a 11 x 21 cm (4¼" x 8¼")strip of navy card. Adhere a photo to the left of this, and, leaving a small border to the right, place a stamped strip.

Stamped title

Top tip

It can be hard achieving a perfectly straight line when using alphabet stamps. Try stamping each letter alternately up, down, up down and keep them close together. This way it looks more interesting and it doesn't matter about the straight line as no one can tell.

4 Trim a 15 x 15 cm (6" x 6") square of patterned paper in yellow and place it toward the bottom of the right side of the first page. To this mount a photo that has a navy mat. Adhere one transparency strip over the top of the photo and one strip below.

5 Cut a 7. 5 x 13 cm (3" x 5¼") strip of green-patterned paper and mat it with a slightly darker shade. Place a mini brad into each of the corners and adhere this to the bottom left of the page over a strip of blue cardstock measuring 7..5 x 10 cm (3" x 4").

6 Crop three photographs, matting two of them, then mount them to the top of the second page and place a stamped strip above and below two of them.

7 Create a pocket using a strip of navy card that measures 11 x 19 cm (4½" x 7½") adhere it on three sides and mount it towards the bottom of the second page. Embellish with a strip of blue cardstock, mini brads and a strip of yellow paper. Put a photo on top, then place a transparency strip over the bottom of the pocket. Cut two green-patterned paper rectangles to desired size and round the corners. Mount these to blue cardstock and round the corners here, too. Use these for extra photos, journaling or memorabilia, then place them into the pocket.

Hidden journaling pocket

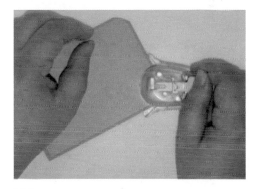

Using a corner rounder

CREATING A TAG ALBUM

Tag albums are a great way to use up left over papers and embellishments. Like the mini albums, they don't take up too much of your time and you can even send them instead of a card.

MATERIALS NEEDED:

Cardstock in shades of blue, green and cream

Patterned papers to complement cardstock and photographs (I used Bo Bunny Press papers and stickers)

A good selection of ribbon

Alphabet stickers

Silver mini brads

Poem stickers

TOOLS NEEDED:

Paper trimmer

Hole punch

Staples

Sandpaper

To begin this project, choose the size of the tag, then make a template out of scrap card. I made mine measure 9 x 16.5 cm (3½" x 6½"). You will then decide on how many pages you wish it to have. I chose eight pages.

1 For the cover, choose the patterned paper and cut out a tag using your template, then punch a hole. Mat a piece of card measuring 5 x 9 cm (2" x 3½") to a piece of card measuring 6 x 9 cm (2½" x 3½"). To change the look of your paper, distress it by sanding it all over, but in particular the edges (you will do this to each page). Mount your sticker alphabet to create the word you wish, then place your sticker poem over a 2 x 7 cm (1"x 2¾") strip. Mount this to your tag using two silver mini brads.

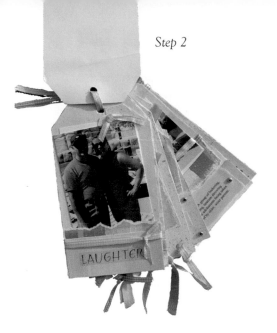

Step 3

Step 4

2 Make a tag using your template on your choice of paper or card, then punch a hole. Cut a 5 x 9 cm (2" x 3½") strip of paper, tear along the top edge, and adhere this to your tag leaving the torn edge unglued so you've created a pocket. Mount a 4 x 9 cm (1½" x 3.½") strip to the pocket and place a poem sticker to it. Wrap a strip of ribbon around the pocket area and tie it with a double knot. Cut two small tags for journaling on and mount them at the top of the tag. Place a photograph within the pocket.

3 Create a tag using your template in your chosen patterned paper, then punch a hole. Cut a piece of patterned paper to 7 x 9 cm (2¾" x 3½"). Mount this to a complementing piece of card leaving a 0.5 cm (¼") border. Wrap a piece of ribbon around the bottom and tie it into a square knot. Mount this leaving a 1 cm (½") border from the bottom of the tag, crop your photo to fit.

4 Make a tag in patterned paper using your template and punch a hole. Cut two 5 x 5 cm (2" x 2") squares, punch a hole at the top and threading a ribbon through each one. Mount them to your tag. Staple a strip of card with your chosen text onto each square tag. Along the bottom of your tag, punch five holes. Thread different ribbons through each one.

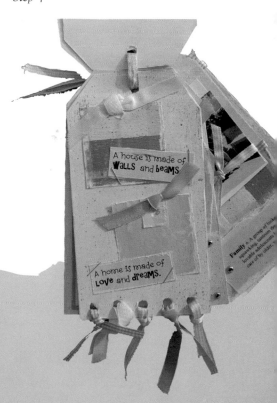

Making a hole.

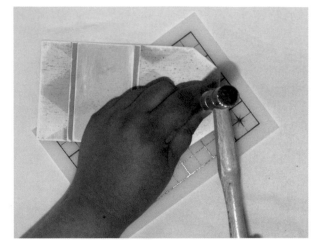

Using stickers.

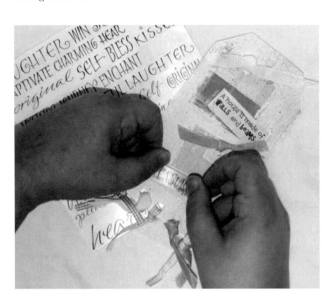

5   Cut a tag using your template, then punch a hole and repeat with a different patterned paper. Then tear approximately 10 cm (4") off the bottom and adhere together. Wrap a ribbon around the top of the tag and tie it into a square knot. Mat your photo, leaving a narrow border and mount to tag.

6   Choose your paper, cut a tag using your template, then punch a hole. Cut a strip of card 5 x 9 cm (2" x 3½") and tear along the top. Place a quote along the centre, then mount to the bottom of your tag to create a pocket. Add a mini silver brad in each corner for decoration. Make two tags measuring 6 x 10 cm (2½" x 4"). Punch out a hole and thread through ribbon. Place a photo onto one small tag and journal on the other, then put them into the pocket.

Step 5

Step 6

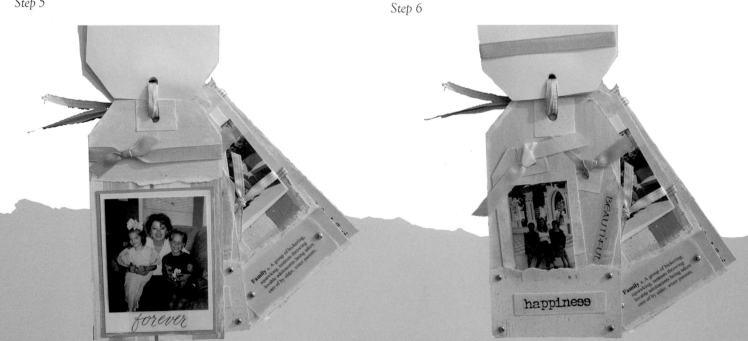

Tying ribbons through tag

7 Using your template and choice of paper, make a tag, then punch a hole. Print some text or use a poem sticker on a 5 x 9 cm (2" x 3½") strip. Tear all four edges off a 4 x 7.5 cm (1.5" x 3") strip and mount on top. Wrap a ribbon just over the top torn edge and tie it into a double knot. Crop your photo to a 3' square and mat it leaving a thin border. Wrap a ribbon around the bottom and tie it with a square knot.

8 Cut a tag using your template, then punch a hole. Cut a 2 x 9 cm (1" x 3") strip of paper and adhere to the left edge centre of tag. Cut a 4 x 6 cm (1¾" x 2½") strip and mount over the smaller strip. Print a verse or use a poem sticker to a 6 x 6 cm (2½") square. Thread a metal-rimmed tag or punch a circle through a strip of ribbon and wrap it around the top of the tag.

Step 7   *Step 8*

7. Gallery section

Use this section to spark your imagination.
You don't have to use exactly the same
colour schemes – change the colours to
complement your own photographs. Add
your own design ideas to create a style that's
uniquely your own. Scrap booking is a
personal thing. If you are happy with the
end result, then that is all that matters.
Over the following pages you will see many
different looks to inspire you in creating
your own scrapbook lay-outs.

Here comes Santa Claus!

SUPPLIES

Cardstock and pattern paper: PTC Company
Stickers: Bo Bunny Press
Pen: Zig writer

Top tip

When using stickers, place them on white cardstock as this will enhance the colours. If you cut around the image when mounted on card you can then position the sticker wherever you would like on the page.

Hero, father, husband

SUPPLIES

Paper: Hot off the press
Embellishments: Hot off the Press and Making Memories
Rubber stamps: Hero Arts

Paper that already has several different designs printed on it, is a great time saver. Use an alphabet stamp set to make your titles. Stagger each letter for a more interesting finish and use the same ink pad to ink around all four sides of the strip.

Muted colours enhance black and white photographs. Mount the buttons using double-sided tape.

By the Sea

SUPPLIES
Cardstock PTC Company
Embellishments: Magic mesh
Brads: Making Memories
Die cuts: My Mind's Eye

These photographs were taken during sunset, giving a silhouette image. A simple layout of plain cardstock with minimal embellishments was all that was needed.

Aber Falls

SUPPLIES
Cardstock: Bazzil
Patterned paper: Bo Bunny
Alphabet stickers: My Mind's Eye
Punch: EK Success

I wanted an outdoor feel to my layout, so I cut three square windows into the borders to place embellishments inside and covered them with coloured vellum for a softer look. When you are using several photos on a page, try matting some with card only, others with several mats of patterned paper and card, and leave some with no mats on at all.

Got Snow

SUPPLIES

Cardstock: PTC Company
Pattern paper: Daisy D
Punches and fibre: EK Success
Pen: Zig writer.

This was a cold snowy day, and I'd made the mistake of allowing the children to snowball me. So, I really wanted to make the photograph the focal point. I wrapped delicate white fibre around the photo giving it added depth.

Bridlington, East Yorkshire

SUPPLIES

Cardstock, stickers: Bo Bunny Press

I love the seaside in the winter with its miles of deserted beaches and brisk winds. A simple colour scheme of red white and blue stripes and plaids, add to the seaside feel. A border created by placing sticker strips over patterned paper is a great way to use up surplus supplies.

Cousins

SUPPLIES
Cardstock: PTC Company
Vellum: Over the Moon Press
Alphabet stickers: EK Success
Beads and buttons: unknown

I placed patterned vellum over my journaling, to give it an underwater feel. The embellishment were kept simple. For a border, beads were threaded onto wire and through the card. Taking inspiration from the water rings, three circles were cut and mounted under a cropped circle photo.

Gone fishin'

SUPPLIES
Cardstock: PTC Company
Pattern paper: Over the Moon Press
Embellishments: Jolees Boutique

One of the easiest ways to change the look of your layout, is to crop a single photo into a shape. Mat your embellishments, as it will emphasise them, and instead of using a paper trimmer to cut your edges, hand cut them with a slightly wavy finish.

Happy Birthday

SUPPLIES

Cardstock: PTC Company
Pattern paper
Stickers: EK Success
Die cuts: Accu cut
Pens: Zig writers

Top tip

Try using coloured pens in a zig-zag pattern to frame your photographs for a totally different look.

Prince

SUPPLIES

Cardstock: Bazzil
Die cuts: Accu cut
Punch: EK Success
Brads: WH Smiths
Pen: Zig opaque writer

I had a hard time finding embellishments for horse riding, so I decided to make my own and created a shaker box filled with punched horse shoes.

To create a shaker box, cut a frame and adhere vellum on the reverse side. Mount foam tape around the entire frame, fill with chosen contents, eg. glitter, beads, punched shapes, etc., and mount card on top to seal it.

Hanging out

SUPPLIES
Cardstock : Bazzil
Patterned paper and transparency: Karen
Foster
Brads: Making Memories
Fibre and ribbons: unknown

The rock pool

SUPPLIES
Cardstock and patterned paper: Cloud 9
Brads: Making Memories
Fibre: Unknown

Top tip

*Place vellum over bright colours: it
will tone them down..*

Ei ei o!

SUPPLIES

Cardstock: PTC company
Magic mesh: Straw

I wanted the feel of the farm on my layout, so I placed strips of straw
onto the magic mesh and made bundles of hay tied together with wire.

Top tip

Make a pocket to hide a special note that you have written. Embellish it by punching holes on either side and tying assorted ribbon and fibres in double knots.

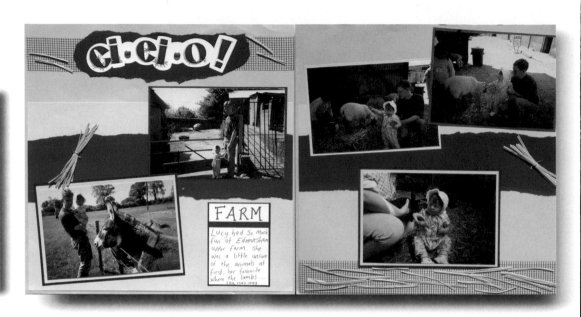

On guard!

SUPPLIES
Cardstock and patterned paper:
PTC company
Stickers: My Minds Eye,
Magic Mesh

Top tip

Use certificates and badges on your layouts as embellishments. On this layout I took a close-up photo of my son in his mask that I cropped and used this for added interest.

Ball pit

SUPPLIES
Cardstock and patterned paper:
PTC company, Magic Mesh
Die-cuts: Accu cut
Pen: Zig writer
Punch: EK Success

Ashton and Chloe just love playing in a ball pit. They would spend all day in one if I'd let them. Because all the photos taken had them both behind the netting, I created a border to look like the ball pit by punching lots of circles in different colours; I stuck them along the bottom of the page, and placed magic mesh over them.

Top tip

Change the colour of your mesh by using an ink pad.

Wonderful brother and sister

SUPPLIES
Cardstock Bazzil Patterned paper: Daisy D
Brads: Making Memories
Stickers: My Mind's Eye

Top tip

If you really want to use a patterned paper, but are finding it too powerful for the photo, try cutting it into different sized sections and place them at intervals on the page.

You are a wonderful brother.

You are so important to our family.

You are a wonderful sister.

Ysgol Feithrin

SUPPLIES
Cardstock and patterned paper: PTC company
Die cuts: Accu cut
Pegs: unknown

If you're like me, then you probably can't bear to throw away any of your children's art work. This was Chloe's first ever picture at pre-school. I made an easel out of black card, mounted the drawing onto white card and placed two pegs at the top.

Top tip
If you can't fit your child's artwork onto a page, take a photo of it, or use a portion of it as a background paper.

Family wedding

SUPPLIES
Cardstock: PTC company
Ribbon: Unknown
Punch: Unknown

Create an unusual border by using ribbon, punch-out shapes in similar shades to the ribbon and mount them in a random pattern.

Puffin island

SUPPLIES

Cardstock Bazzil Patterned paper: Daisy D
Brads and eyelets: Making Memories
Rubber stamps: Hero Arts

I wanted a special embellishment for my tag,
so I scanned the photo image, enlarged it and
printed it onto vellum.

Sister Brother

SUPPLIES

Cardstock: PTC company
Patterned paper: Daisy D, Bo Bunny Press
Transparency: Daisy D

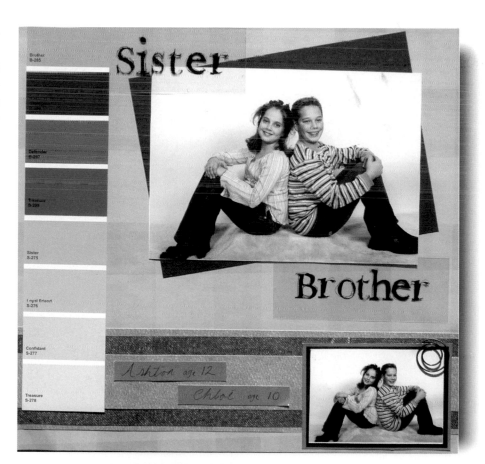

Bronte Parsonage

SUPPLIES

Cardstock: Bazzil

Stickers: PSX

Top tip

Use postcards on your layouts as embellishments. If you are worried about them not being acid-free, scan them into your computer and print them out or mat them with acid- and lignin-free card.

Grow

SUPPLIES
Cardstock: [need text]
Patterned paper: [need text]
Transparency: [need text]

Top tip

Use paint colour samples as embellishments on your layouts. Print words or verses onto each colour.

A family is love

SUPPLIES

Cardstock vellum and patterned paper: PTC company

Die cut: Sissix

Buttons: unknown

Top tip

Use a sheet of A4 patterned paper on a 12" x 12" page, by tearing approximately a third. Place the larger section to the left or right of the page and mount the smaller piece to the opposite side.

Glossary

ACID-FREE – Any material that ranges from 7.0–9.0 on the pH scale at the time of its manufacture. These products have been determined to be 'acid-free', therefore making them safe to use with your photographs and memorabilia.

ADHESIVE – A substance used to bond materials together. In scrapbooking there are many types of adhesives used, including glue sticks, tape guns, sprays, dots, double-sided tape, etc. Many of these come in either a permanent or repositional bond, depending on your needs.

ALTERED – Using scrapbooking products and techniques to alter an item such as a book, paint can, CD, clip board etc.

ARCHIVAL – Materials that are considered suitable for long term storage and preservation purposes.

BACKGROUND PAPER – The base or bottom layer of card or paper in a completed scrapbook page.

BORDERS – The outermost edges of your layout. Many are decorated using chalks, paints, sculpting scissors.

BRAD – Two of the main uses for brads are fastening and embellishing. They come in many shapes, sizes, colours, etc. Bendable metal nibs/prongs are attached to the bottom of a brad. When pushed through paper they can be bent outwards to fix in place.

CARDSTOCK – Firm and sturdy paper. The base of most scrapbook pages to which papers and embellishments are adhered. Cardstock comes in many weights, sizes and textures.

COLOUR WHEEL – A circular diagram in which primary and usually intermediate colours are arranged sequentially, so that related colours are next to each. Used to create 'colour schemes'.

CHALK / CHALKING – Acid-free decorating chalks are perfect for embellishing die cuts, stencilling, drawing and shading. They're fun and easy to use. Excellent for rubber stamp, scrapbooks and other projects.

CIRCLE JOURNAL (CJ) – Usually a themed album passed around a group of people, who each add one page of their own design and then pass it to another in the group until completed.

COLLAGE – An artistic composition of objects pasted or glued over a surface, made of layers of materials, often with unifying lines and colour. Known as a 'style' in scrapbooking.

COLOUR BLOCKING – Technique of getting a balanced look on your pages by using blocks of various coloured paper to create layout backgrounds. Many ready made 'colour blocking' templates are available in the market.

CROP – Simply means to cut or trim. Also used as another term for a scrapbook workshop.

DIE-CUTS – Shapes made from paper or cardstock, created by using a die-cut machine. Many 'home' versions of die-cutting systems are available in the marketplace.

EMBELLISHMENT – Products used to decorate or enhance a page layout. Embellishments include, stickers, brads, eyelets, tags, buttons, etc.

EPHEMERA – A short-lived event represented on printed materials. In scrapbooking refers mainly to items such as cancelled stamps, ticket stubs, postcards, etc.

EYELET – In scrapbooking eyelets are used for both decoration and fastening. They come in a variety of shapes, colours and sizes. They are set in place using an 'eyelet setter'.

FIBRES – Threads used to decorate scrapbook pages. Their design varies from simple to very fancy.

FOCAL POINT – The place on a scrapbook page that the eye is naturally drawn to. In scrapbooking the 'focal point' is usually the main photograph on the page.

INKING – Using ink to add accents to pages. Some techniques include, smearing, staining and smudging. Inking is usually used around the edges of objects but can be used throughout a layout as needed.

JOURNALING – The written words on a scrapbook page.

LAYOUT – A scrapbook page is generally called a 'layout'. Also used as a term for organising a page beforehand.

LIGNIN – A compound that hardens and strengthens the cell walls of plants. Considered to cause degradation if present during the final stages of paper manufacture.

MATTING / PHOTO MATTING – Building up a background for a photograph to be placed on. Generally more than two layers are used and will be slightly larger than the photo giving it a framed look.

MEMORABILIA – Special objects of past events, used to enhance or feature in a layout such as souvenirs and items from holidays, etc.

MINI-ALBUM – A scaled down version of a full-sized album. They can either be homemade or purchased in many colours and sizes.

MOSAIC – A decorative design made by cutting small pieces of paper or photographs, and placing them on a page, thus creating a 'mosaic' look.

MOUNT: – To attach or adhere an object, usually a photograph, to a piece of card or paper.

PAGE PROTECTORS/SHEET PROTECTORS – Acid-free plastic sheets or 'pockets' used to store and protect scrapbook pages.

PAPER PIECING – Cutting out shapes to create a picture which can be used as decoration for a layout, or can be the entire layout itself.

PAPER TEARING – Used to create a unique textured look, as opposed to simply cutting with scissors or trimmers.

PAPER TRIMMERS/CUTTERS – A paper cutter designed to cut straight lines. Some trimmers come with interchangeable blades, which allow decorative edges rather than just a straight cut.

PATTERNED PAPER – Sometimes called 'designer' paper. Paper with designs printed on surfaces. 1000's of different colours and designs are available.

PERSONAL DIE-CUTTING SYSTEMS – Cutting systems designed for home use. Generally smaller and lighter than industrial models.

PH LEVEL – The measurement of acidity/alkalinity. A pH balanced paper is considered to have a pH level of 7.

PHOTO SAFE – Products that are safe to use with photos.

POCKETS – Used to hold items such as tags, photos, and memorabilia. Generally made using paper, fabric and vellum.

POLYPROPYLENE – Plastics considered safe for photographs.

PVC – Polyvinylchloride is a common thermoplastic resin that emits hydrochloric acid, that can easily damage paper-based products.

RUB-ON TRANSFERS – Products designed to be applied to surfaces by rubbing them on. Usually accomplished by rubbing a flat wooden stick on the back of a transfer surface.

SCRAPLIFTING – Using previously created layouts from others for inspiration on personal projects.

SCRAPPER'S BLOCK – A creative block when trying to come up with ideas for layouts.

SHABBY CHIC – Method used to create a worn or used look. Can be accomplished by scrunching and sanding your papers.

THEME – The overall flavour of a page or layout

TRANSPARENCY – A clear film with various designs printed on it. Used to lay over another surface, allowing you to see through to the page below.

VELLUM – Semi-clear paper, similar to tracing paper you may have used as a child.

Index

Credits

Thank you to Anson, Ashton and Chloe my wonderful family for putting up with all the late nights, long weekends and takeouts. I couldn't do what I do without your support.

Mum, Dad, Melanie, Nadine, Linsey and Nathan for always believing in me even when I know you thought I was away with the fairies.

Sue and Richard, Bubba and Zell, for all the encouragement, and no-nonsense straight Yorkshire talk, 'it's gonna be great'.

Joanne, Jane, Cheryl, Kirsty and Mary Anne for being such great and amazingly talented friends; a big thank you for every thing.

Julie, the Yorkshire lass in Dallas, you are an inspiration.

Rob you are my right-hand man in so many of my projects: thank you.

There have been many people who have touched my life in the crafting world and have become an inspiration and friend, far to many to mention by name. A few who have always been there to inspire or just to natter include: Alan, Barry, Rachel, Elaine, Mark, Shelly, Julie, Heather, Corinne, Sarah, Lynn, Shimelle, Kathleen, Suzanne and Darwin.

A big thank you to each and every one of you who buys this book. I hope you all enjoy it and it gives you the inspiration to take more photos, tell a story and create your very own scrapbooks.

About the author

Jayne Bentley owns The Paper Trail Scrapbook Company, which supplies thousands of scrapbooking products to people all over the world, via the internet, mail order and the retail shop in Bridlington, England.

Jayne is a designer and has her own range of rubber stamps, "little rascals" scrapbook albums, storage system and templates, "cool memories" and design embellishments, paper, card and cut-out ranges for American and British companies.

Jayne contributes to several craft magazines and has appeared on QVC; she makes regular appearances on Ideal World and Create and Craft television shows demonstrating scrapbooking. She also demonstrates throughout the UK, Europe and the USA.

Jayne lives with her husband Anson, her son Ashton and her daughter Chloe, in Bridlington East Yorkshire.